I0407887

Master Mandalas

Copyright: Published in the United States by Christopher Bollinger
Published January 2017
ISBN-13: 978-1542679886
ISBN-10: 1542679885

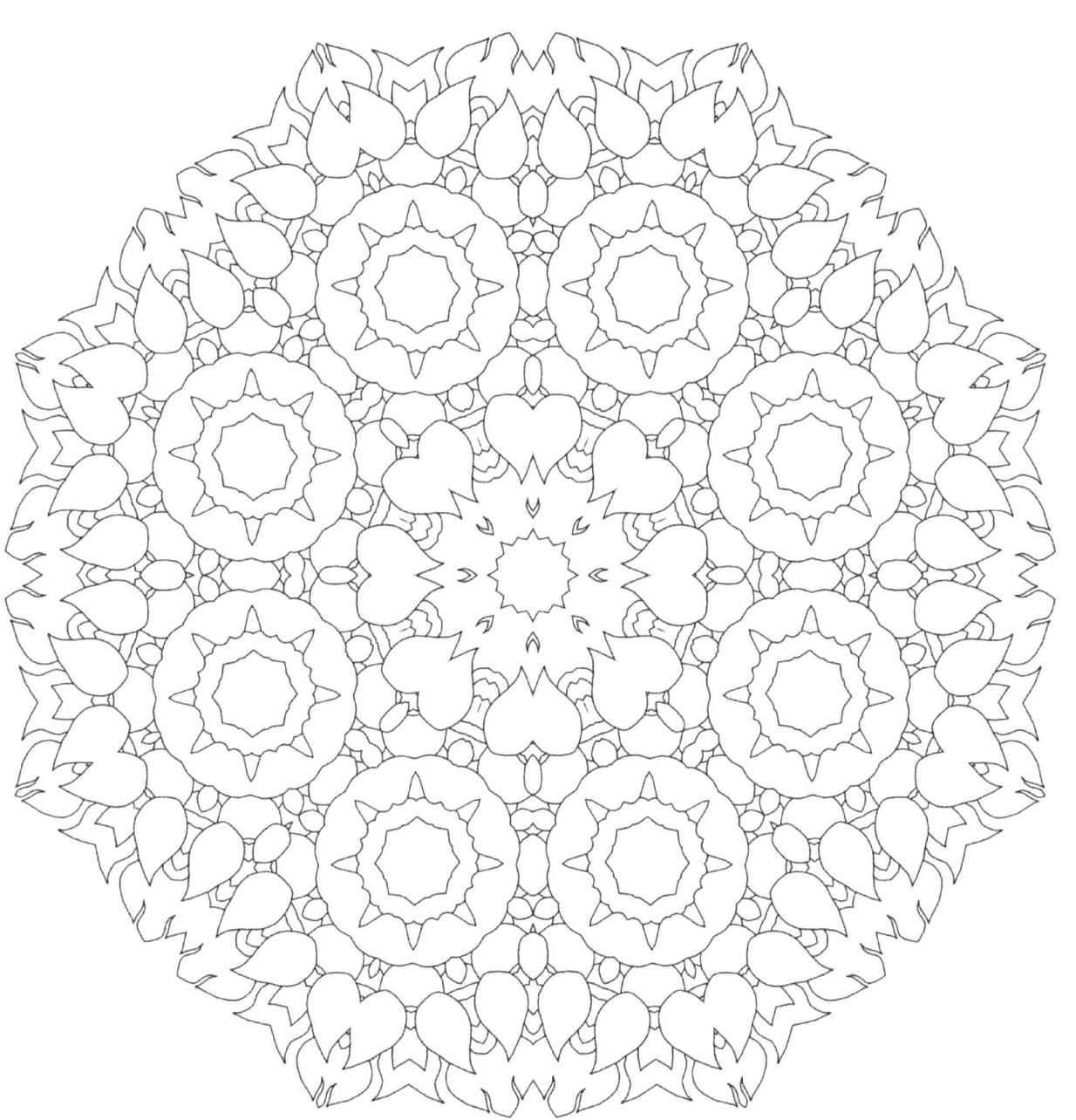

Thank you

www.ingramcontent.com/pod-product-compliance
Lightning Source LLC
Chambersburg PA
CBHW081555280526
45788CB00011B/3480